This book is a confirmation gift to

D1529343

Through St. Peter, God says to all Christians: "But you are a chosen people, a royal priesthood, a holy nation, a people belonging to God, that you may declare the praises of Him who called you out of darkness into His wonderful light. Once you were not a people, but now you are the people of God; once you had not received mercy, but now you have received mercy" (1 Peter 2:9–10).

May this book build up your faith and provide guidance for your Christian life. May you always rejoice in being one of God's own people and declare His wonderful deeds.

Yours in Christian love,

....

Signed

....

Date

Confirmation Remembered

CONCORDIA PUBLISHING HOUSE · SAINT LOUIS

	3	4	5	6	7	8	9	10	11
13	12	11	10	09	08	07	06	05	

Your Confirmation Day

As a child of God, you have two birthdays. The first is the day of your birth into the world. The second is the day of your birth into the church. Some time after your first birth-day you were baptized and became a member of the body of Christ.

You may not remember the day of your Baptism. Your sponsors spoke for the faith the Holy Spirit had planted in your heart long before you were able to speak of it yourself. In order that you might confirm publicly what they promised years ago, the church has instituted the Rite of Confirmation. With your own lips you repeated the solemn vows spoken for you at your Baptism.

It is a day to be remembered always, for it is a beginning, not an end. As you make your way through life, there will be thousands of voices trying to tell you to forget your vows. There will be sin and temptation. The world outside of your church will try to persuade you to forget the promises you made at your confirmation.

But you will remember! You will remember the long hours of preparation for the brief moment in your confirmation service when you stood and took your place beside your Savior forever. You will remember the voice of your pastor reminding you to remain faithful unto death.

And whenever sin, trouble, or temptation in your life threaten to make you forget this day, you will run to Him who said: "I will never leave you or forsake you." He will be forever where He was on the day of your confirmation, near you with the crown of life in His nail-scarred hands.

Pray

Lord Jesus, I thank You for making me Your child through my Baptism. Keep me always close to You so I may never forget Your love for me in bringing me into Your kingdom. Give me grace to remember the day when I stood before You and my church and promised to be faithful to You always. For Your name's sake. Amen.

. . . .

And we know that in all things God works for the good of those who love Him, who have been called according to His purpose. Romans 8:28

. . . .

My Confirmation Vow

"Do you intend to continue steadfast in this confession and Church and to suffer all, even death, rather than fall away from it?"

"I do so intend with the help of God."

"Do you hold the prophetic and apostolic Scriptures to be the inspired Word of God and confess the doctrine of the Evangelical Lutheran Church, drawn from them, as you have learned to know it from the Small Catechism, to be faithful and true?"

"I do."

"Do you desire to become a member of the Evangelical Lutheran Church and of this congregation?"

"I do."

"Do you intend faithfully to conform all your life to the divine Word, to be faithful in the use of God's Word and Sacraments, which are His means of grace, and in faith, word, and action to remain true to God, Father, Son, and Holy Spirit, even to death?"

"I do so intend by the grace of God."

(Lutheran Worship, p. 206)

My Confirmation Day

What one memory stands out from your confirmation day? How was it a special day for you?

....

....

....

....

....

....

....

....

....

....

....

....

Hard Questions

Isn't faith really my decision? Don't I have to do something? In other words, don't I have to decide to believe in Jesus?

It might seem—on the surface—that we have a decision to make about our faith. God's Word, however, paints a different picture.

First, God "wants all men to be saved and come to a knowledge of the truth" (1 Timothy 2:4). The Holy Spirit is willing and able to work faith in everyone. When you witness to a friend about Jesus and your friend believes, it's clear proof: the Holy Spirit has worked faith.

You, as a witness to Christ, were the instrument God's Spirit used to bring the Gospel into another person's life.

Faith is God's goal and gift.

If your friend does not believe, it's not because the Spirit has refused to work. It's not because God does not want your friend to know Christ and His salvation. We can't decide on our own to believe in Jesus as our Savior, but we can decide to reject Him. Perhaps your friend has chosen to reject God's gift.

Check it Out! Hebrews 11 gives a great definition and many examples of faith in God's promises. Write your own definition of faith in Jesus as Lord and Savior.

. . . .

. . . .

. . . .

. . . .

. . . .

. . . .

. . . .

. . . .

. . . .

. . . .

. . . .

Let Us Ever Walk with Jesus

Let us ever walk with Jesus,
Follow His example pure,
Through a world that would deceive us
And to sin our spirits lure.
Onward in His footsteps treading,
Pilgrims here, our home above,
Full of faith and hope and love,
Let us do our Father's bidding.
Faithful Lord, with me abide;
I shall follow where You guide.

(Lutheran Worship, 386)

Confirmation Remembered

Check it Out! Read 1 Thessalonians 4:1–7.

Summarize, in your own words, God's will for believers.

....

....

....

....

....

....

....

....

....

....

....

God's Word

The Bible is our source book, our reference. If you want to know the truth about God, you start with the Bible.

- *Bible* means "book"

- *Holy* means "sacred," "set apart," or "perfect."

- The Holy Bible is God's sacred, perfect book— His Word for human beings.

God's Word tells what God wants us to know.

- The Bible is true. It contains no lies or untruths.

- The Bible is inspired. God guided the writers in what they wrote and how they wrote it. *Inspired* means that God "breathed into" the writers to give His Word.

- The Bible is trustworthy. You can trust everything it has to say. It will not deceive or lead you down the wrong path.

The Old Testament has 39 books and is divided into 5 main sections:

- 5 books of the *law*—Genesis, Exodus, Leviticus, Numbers, Deuteronomy

- 12 books of *history*—Joshua, Judges, Ruth, 1 Samuel, 2 Samuel, 1 Kings, 2 Kings, 1 Chronicles, 2 Chronicles, Ezra, Nehemiah, Esther

- 5 books of *poetry*—Job, Psalms, Proverbs, Ecclesiastes, Song of Songs

- 5 *major prophets*—Isaiah, Jeremiah, Lamentations, Ezekiel, Daniel

- 12 *minor prophets*—Hosea, Joel, Amos, Obadiah, Jonah, Micah, Nahum, Habakkuk, Zephaniah, Haggai, Zechariah, Malachi

The New Testament has 27 books and 5 divisions:

- 4 *gospels*—Matthew, Mark, Luke, John

- 1 book of *history*—The Acts of the Apostles

- 13 *epistles* (letters) of St. Paul—Romans, 1 Corinthians, 2 Corinthians, Galatians, Ephesians, Philippians, Colossians, 1 Thessalonians, 2 Thessalonians, 1 Timothy, 2 Timothy, Titus, Philemon

- 8 *general epistles* (letters)—Hebrews, James, 1 Peter, 2 Peter, 1 John, 2 John, 3 John, Jude

- 1 book of *prophecy*—Revelation

Thy Strong Word

Thy strong word did cleave the darkness;
At Thy speaking it was done.
For created light we thank Thee,
While Thine ordered seasons run.
Alleluia, alleluia!
Praise to Thee who light dost send!
Alleluia, alleluia!
Alleluia without end!

Give us lips to sing Thy glory,
Tongues Thy mercy to proclaim,
Throats that shout the hope that fills us,
Mouths to speak Thy holy name.
Alleluia, alleluia!
May the light which Thou dost send
Fill our songs with alleluias,
Alleluias without end!

(Lutheran Worship, 328)

Confirmation Remembered

God's Word

The Old Testament points to Christ. We refer to the Old Testament era as B.C. ("Before Christ").

The New Testament starts with Christ. The time after Christ's birth is termed A.D., from the Latin words, *Anno Domini* ("In the year of our Lord").

The Old Testament was written in Hebrew, the language of God's chosen people, Israel.

The New Testament was written in Greek, the language commonly spoken at the time of Christ.

It took 1,000 years to assemble the Old Testament (1500–500 B.C.).

It took 50 years to assemble the New Testament (A.D. 45–95).

Why does God give the Bible?

God wants all people to know that

- we need a Savior,

- He has provided that Savior in Jesus,

- we can enjoy His blessings of forgiveness and eternal life forever.

What should we do with the Bible?

- Read it.

- Study it. Learn what it has to say.

- Hear it preached and explained.

- Believe it.

- Live it. Do what it says.

- Share it with others.

Check it Out! Read 2 Peter 1:20–21.

What does St. Peter mean?

....

....

....

....

....

....

....

....

....

....

....

Hard Questions!

I read the Bible and sometimes it doesn't make much sense. Why are there all those lists of people with strange names? What about all the "sex and violence" in certain books? What does this have to do with my life?

It is true that some things in the Bible may be hard to understand. We may not always understand why God put some stories in His book.

Why, for example, are all those sins of great people included? In one sense, that one's easy. When we understand that even the greatest people of faith were sinners and God still forgave them, then we can be assured that God loves us, cares about us, and forgives and takes care of us.

Lists of names can be difficult to read through, too. But the Bible's lists—often called genealogies—show God's love and care for His world and His chosen people throughout history. In those lists you can see the names of people who received the promises, believed them, and passed them on to family and neighbors. Jesus is the center of God's promises. From generation to generation, God fulfilled His Word by working to bring His salvation in Christ to all nations.

What is important whenever you read the Bible is to recognize and understand God's Good News of salvation in Jesus Christ!

Isn't it Curious? God put the whole Gospel in one sentence in the Bible. Read and reflect on John 3:16.

....

....

....

....

....

....

....

....

....

....

....

....

Beautiful Savior

Beautiful Savior,
King of creation,
Son of God and Son of Man!
Truly I'd love Thee,
Truly I'd serve Thee,
Light of my soul, my joy, my crown.

Fair are the meadows,
Fair are the woodlands,
Robed in flow'rs of blooming spring;
Jesus is fairer,
Jesus is purer,
He makes our sorr'wing spirit sing.

Fair is the sunshine,
Fair is the moonlight,
Bright the sparkling stars on high;
Jesus shines brighter,
Jesus shines purer
Than all the angels in the sky.

Beautiful Savior,
Lord of the nations,
Son of God and Son of Man!
Glory and honor,
Praise, adoration
Now and forevermore be Thine!

(Lutheran Worship, 507)

Confirmation Remembered

What Do You Think?

The Bible reveals important truths about God. What do you learn from these passages?

Psalm 118:1

....

Psalm 145:9

....

Jeremiah 3:12

....

Titus 3:5

....

Exodus 34:6–7

....

1 John 4:8

....

John 4:24

....

Psalm 90:1–2

....

Psalm 102:27

....

Malachi 3:6

....

Genesis 17:1

....

Matthew 19:26

....

John 21:17

....

Acts 17:27

....

Leviticus 19:2

....

Deuteronomy 32:4

....

2 Timothy 2:13

....

Read John 17:17. What does Jesus say about God's Word? What does this mean for you?

....

....

....

....

....

....

....

....

....

....

....

....

Where to Find

Unless I am convinced
by the testimony of Holy Scripture,
. . . I cannot and will not recant,
since it is neither safe nor advisable to
do anything against conscience.
Here I stand;
I cannot do otherwise!
God help me. Amen.

Martin Luther, 1521

My Favorite Bible Passages

....

....

....

....

....

....

....

....

....

....

....

....

....

Prayer

God wants us to talk to Him, to tell Him our concerns, to share our joys, to reflect on our faith.

God invites us to pray. What a privilege and opportunity!

There is no limit to how much we can pray, what we can pray about, how often we can pray. We can take absolutely "everything" to the Lord in prayer.

No, in all these things
we are more than conquerors
through Him who loved us.
For I am convinced that
neither death nor life,
neither angels nor demons,
neither the present nor the future,
nor any powers, neither height nor
depth, nor anything else in all creation,
will be able to separate us from
the love of God that is in
Christ Jesus our Lord.
Romans 8:37–39

Prayer is

- a heart-to-heart talk with God;

- a quiet reflection in heart and mind;

- an act of adoration, confession, thanks-giving, and request, alone and with other believers.

To whom do we pray?

- To God alone! Our gracious Father invites us to come directly to Him with every concern and need, thanksgiving and praise.

For what should we pray?

There's really no limit.

Pray for:

- spiritual blessings
  (faith, obedience to God's Word).

Ask that God's will be done to meet our:

- physical and personal needs
  (health and healing);

- earthly needs
  (shelter, food, clothes, family, friends);

- human conditions
  (injustice, war, hunger, poverty).

God Bless Our Native Land

God bless our native land;
Firm may it ever stand
Through storm and night.
When the wild tempests rave,
Ruler of wind and wave,
Do Thou our country save
By Thy great might.

So shall our prayers arise
To God above the skies;
On Him we wait.
Thou who art ever nigh,
Guarding with watchful eye,
To Thee aloud we cry:
God save the state!

(*Lutheran Worship*, 497)

When and where should we pray?

- Again, there's no limit.
  God is ready to listen whenever you pray.

- Morning, evening, at meals

- Times of special needs

- Times of special thanksgiving

- At church

- In our homes; in our rooms

- At school or on the job

- By ourselves and with our family
  and friends

- On the athletic field, taking a hike

- Anytime

. . . .

Therefore I tell you,
whatever you ask for in prayer,
believe that you have received it,
and it will be yours.
Mark 11:24

. . . .

What prayers should I use?

- The Lord's Prayer is called the perfect model prayer.

- Your own prayer, in your own words.

- The church has a lot of traditional prayers that are beautiful expressions of faith. They can still be helpful.

- There are lots of prayer books in print, written for all ages and personal circumstances.

*I'm not good at praying in front of people.
What can I do?*

Prayer is between you and God. That's all that matters. It's not for public display. Remember the story of the Pharisee and the Publican. Sure there are people who are eloquent prayers. They have a wonderful way with words. Their prayers are beautiful. But you don't have to pray like those people to be heard.

Just let God know what's on your heart. Sometimes you may not even be able to find the words, and you end up by saying something such as "God, You know the need. Please help."

No one should be made to pray. Requiring everyone to say something can make a prayer a self-righteous act. Sometimes it feels like the good prayers get Brownie points. A "popcorn" prayer is not bad. It gives everyone who wants to pray the opportunity to do so. But no one is made to pray.

Praying should never make a person feel uncomfortable. If you find yourself feeling uncomfortable when praying in groups, you may want to speak to your leader. You won't be alone.

Finally, maybe it sounds a little strange, but you may want to pray about it. God can help with this concern, too.

What Wondrous Love Is This

What wondrous love is this, O my soul, O my soul!
What wondrous love is this, O my soul!
What wondrous love is this
That caused the Lord of bliss
To bear the dreadful curse for my soul, for my soul,
To bear the dreadful curse for my soul!

When I was sinking down, sinking down, sinking down,
When I was sinking down, sinking down,
When I was sinking down
Beneath God's righteous frown,
Christ laid aside His crown for my soul, for my soul,
Christ laid aside His crown for my soul.

To God and to the Lamb I will sing, I will sing;
To God and to the Lamb I will sing;
To God and to the Lamb,
Who is the great I AM,
While millions join the theme, I will sing, I will sing,
While millions join the theme, I will sing.

And when from death I'm free, I'll sing on, I'll sing on;
And when from death I'm free, I'll sing on.
And when from death I'm free
I'll sing His love for me,
And through eternity I'll sing on, I'll sing on,
And through eternity I'll sing on.

(Hymnal Supplement 98, 860)

You may find it helpful to start a prayer journal. Keep a notebook handy and jot down your thoughts and prayers. You may find that writing prayers helps you find the words. The journal also becomes a record of your prayer journey, and you can see how God has answered you.

....

I no longer call you servants,
because a servant does not know
his master's business.
Instead, I have called you friends,
for everything that I learned from
My Father I have made known to you.
You did not choose me,
but I chose you and appointed you to go
and bear fruit—fruit that will last.
Then the Father will give you whatever
you ask in My name.
John 15:15–16

....

How does God answer prayer?

- With *Yes.* He grants what we ask.

- With *No.* He has other ideas.

- With *Wait.* He may want us to take some time to review our request, to reflect on His grace, to see His will. His answers don't always come immediately. But He does answer, and His answers are always right.

Why say "Amen"?

- *Amen* means "It shall be so." At the end of a prayer, it indicates we believe that we have been heard.

Check it Out! Read 1 Thessalonians 5:16–18.

What does St. Paul say about prayer? How could this influence your prayer life?

....

....

....

....

....

....

....

....

....

....

....

Hard Questions!

Can I Pray in School?

Absolutely! There's no rule that says you cannot. If you are taking a test, there's no reason you can't or shouldn't ask for guidance and strength. Your prayer is between you and God.

Many people get upset about prayer in public schools when prayers or "moments of silence" are mandatory, that is, required by law or school. The United States of America has a rich tradition of religious freedom, freedom to both worship according to one's beliefs and practices and to be free from government intervention and regulation.

It's possible that mandatory public prayers in public schools could include prayers to false gods from false religions. Christians don't want to be involved in these kinds of prayer. Often prayer in public is best left for individuals to do in silence.

Read Romans 8:26–27. What does St. Paul say about the Holy Spirit and our prayers? What reassurance does this give you?

....

....

....

....

....

....

....

....

....

....

....

Luther's Morning Prayer

I thank You, my heavenly Father, through Jesus Christ, Your dear Son, that You have kept me safe this night from all harm and danger; and I pray that You would keep me this day also from sin and every evil, that all my doings and life may please You. For into Your hands I commend myself, my body and soul, and all things. Let Your holy angel be with me, that the evil foe may have no power over me. Amen.

(*Luther's Small Catechism with Explanation*, p. 30)

Luther's Evening Prayer

I thank You, my heavenly Father, through Jesus Christ, Your dear Son, that You have graciously kept me this day; and I pray that You would forgive me all my sins where I have done wrong, and graciously keep me this night. For into Your hands I commend myself, my body and soul, and all things. Let Your holy angel be with me, that the evil foe may have no power over me. Amen.

(Luther's Small Catechism with Explanation, p. 31)

Asking a Blessing

Lord God, heavenly Father, bless us and these Your gifts which we receive from Your bountiful goodness, through Jesus Christ, our Lord. Amen.

(Luther's Small Catechism with Explanation, p. 32)

Returning Thanks

We thank You, Lord God, heavenly Father, for all Your benefits, through Jesus Christ, our Lord, who lives and reigns with You and the Holy Spirit forever and ever. Amen.

(*Luther's Small Catechism with Explanation*, p. 32)

Worship

It's a simple fact: God designed a seven-day week, with one day set aside for rest and worship. The day of rest and worship is called the Sabbath. It is a day to rest, put aside your labors, and let your body rest, renew, and revive.

God is our model. He rested from six days of creation labor.

In the Old Testament, the children of Israel were commanded to worship on the seventh day.

In the New Testament, we are commanded to worship, but the day is not specified.

Christians have traditionally worshiped on Sunday because

- it's the day of Christ's resurrection;

- it's the day on which God began His creation;

- the Holy Spirit founded the New Testament church on Pentecost, a Sunday.

Sunday morning is the day and time usually set aside for worship, but ...

In today's world, many churches offer alternatives to Sunday morning worship. How about Saturday night? Sunday night? Monday night? You could probably find some church somewhere in worship any day or night of the week.

. . . .

Let the word of Christ
dwell in you richly as you teach
and admonish one another with
all wisdom, and as you sing psalms,
hymns and spiritual songs with gratitude
in your hearts to God.
And whatever you do, whether in word
or deed, do it all in the name of the
Lord Jesus, giving thanks to God the
Father through Him.
Colossians 3:16–17

. . . .

Many people ask the question, "Do I have to go to church?"

In one sense, the answer is probably no. Salvation is not dependent on your church and Sunday school attendance record. What is necessary is faith in Jesus Christ as Lord and Savior.

On the other hand, the question is really selfish and misguided. It's not a question that comes from a strong faith. Sure, Sunday morning worship will not be a mountaintop experience every time. Perhaps church can, on occasion, seem a little boring or unrelated to everyday life.

At the same time, though, God's Word encourages us to gather regularly for worship and study.

> "Let us not give up meeting together, as some are in the habit of doing, but let us encourage one another— and all that more as you see the Day approaching." Hebrews 10:25

When we gather for worship, God blesses the time we spend with Him.

- We hear of His love and mercy through Jesus Christ in His Word.

- Through the Gospel and the Sacraments, we receive the forgiveness of sins Jesus earned for us through His life, death, and resurrection.

- We rejoice in the community of saints—believers—who await the blessings of eternal life with the Lord Jesus.

The blessings we receive in worship are simply great. Why would anyone want to miss the opportunity?

Draw Near and Take the Body of the Lord

Draw near and take the body of the Lord,
And drink the holy blood for you outpoured;
Offered was He for greatest and for least,
Himself the victim and Himself the priest.

He who His saints in this world rules and shields,
To all believers life eternal yields;
With heav'nly bread He makes the hungry whole,
Gives living waters to the thirsting soul.

Come forward then with faithful hearts sincere,
And take the pledges of salvation here.
O Lord, our hearts with grateful thanks endow
As in this feast of love You bless us now.

(Lutheran Worship, 240)

Check it Out! Read Hebrews 10:25.

What does God encourage in His Word?

....

....

....

....

....

....

....

....

....

....

....

Sing to the LORD
you saints of His;
praise His holy name.
Psalm 30:4

Hard Questions

What about the day of "rest"? Can I do anything on Sunday?

God rested, that is, stopped His creative work, on the seventh day. In this way He gives an example for His creation. God knows our need to refresh and renew our lives. He provides a day of rest because He loves and desires to preserve human beings.

Some people "play" as hard on the Sabbath as they work the rest of the week. Their bodies and minds never get a chance to rest and repair. They may always be tired.

The Sabbath rest gets you ready for the week's work ahead. Resting is good stewardship of the body, mind, and spirit that God has given you. Who can argue with that?

Oh, Come, All Ye Faithful

Oh, come, all ye faithful,
Joyful and triumphant!
Oh, come ye, oh, come ye to Bethlehem;
Come and behold Him
Born the King of angels:

Refrain
   Oh, come, let us adore Him,
   Oh, come, let us adore Him,
   Oh, come, let us adore Him,
   Christ the Lord!

Highest, most holy,
Light of light eternal,
Born of a virgin, a mortal He comes;
Son of the Father
Now in flesh appearing!

Refrain

Sing, choirs of angels,
Sing in exultation,
Sing, all ye citizens of heaven above!
Glory to God
In the highest:

Refrain

Yea, Lord, we greet Thee,
Born this happy morning;
Jesus, to Thee be glory giv'n!
Word of the Father,
Now in flesh appearing!

Refrain

(Lutheran Worship, 41)

At the Lamb's High Feast We Sing

At the Lamb's high feast we sing
Praise to our victorious King,
Who has washed us in the tide
Flowing from His pierced side.
Alleluia!

Praise we Him, whose love divine
Gives His sacred blood for wine,
Gives His body for the feast—
Christ the victim, Christ the priest.
Alleluia!

Where the paschal blood is poured,
Death's dread angel sheathes the sword;
Israel's hosts triumphant go
Through the wave that drowns the foe.
Alleluia!

Praise we Christ, whose blood was shed,
Paschal victim, paschal bread;
With sincerity and love
Eat we manna from above.
Alleluia!

Mighty Victim from the sky,
Hell's fierce pow'rs beneath You lie;
You have conquered in the fight,
You have brought us life and light.
Alleluia!

Now no more can death appall,
Now no more the grave enthrall;
You have opened paradise,
And Your saints in You shall rise.
Alleluia!

Easter triumph, Easter joy!
This alone can sin destroy;
From sin's pow'r, Lord, set us free,
Newborn souls in You to be.
Alleluia!

Father, who the crown shall give,
Savior, by whose death we live,
Spirit, guide through all our days:
Three in One, Your name we praise.
Alleluia!

(*Lutheran Worship*, 126)

Tell about a particular worship service that had a special meaning for you. Why was it special?

....

....

....

....

....

....

....

....

....

....

....

....

....

Me

Human beings are the "brightest and best" of all God's visible creatures. Humans are, in fact, made in God's image and likeness (Genesis 1:27). We are special and unique. No other creatures are like us. We are different from the rest of the animal world because …

- We can speak. We have a language.

- We can use our minds to think and reason. Animals have instinct but they cannot differentiate between cause and effect. Human beings can make decisions.

- Human beings have an immortal soul. That means we live forever. God's original plan was for us to live with Him forever in paradise.

- We walk upright.

- We have a specific job. We are given dominion over the earth. In other words, we are in charge and responsible for taking care of God's creation.

- We are intended to be holy like God. That's a part of God's image.

Because we were made in God's image and likeness, Adam and Eve's wills ran parallel with God's will. What God wanted Adam and Eve also wanted.

Sin destroyed the unity between God and human beings. For all practical purposes, we lost the divine image. The human will now runs counter to God's will.

On earth, we will never regain God's perfect image. But thanks be to God through Jesus Christ our Lord! God works out our salvation in Jesus. We will be fully restored to God's glory in heaven!

Check it Out! Read Numbers 6:24–26.

What blessings does God give to His people?
What does this mean for you?

. . . .

. . . .

. . . .

. . . .

. . . .

. . . .

. . . .

. . . .

. . . .

. . . .

. . . .

. . . .

"For I know the plans
I have for you,"
declares the LORD,
plans to prosper you
and not to harm you,
plans to give you hope
and a future."
Jeremiah 29:11

In what ways has God made you unique?
List 5–10 specific traits about yourself—your looks,
talents, interests, or goals—that describe who you are
by God's design.

. . . .

. . . .

. . . .

. . . .

. . . .

. . . .

. . . .

. . . .

. . . .

. . . .

. . . .

. . . .

Read Galatians 5:22–23. Write out the "fruit of the Spirit." What fruit of the Spirit do you see in your life?

....

....

....

....

....

....

....

....

....

....

....

....

....

I am Jesus' Little Lamb

I am Jesus' little lamb,
Ever glad at heart I am;
For my Shepherd gently guides me,
Knows my need and well provides me,
Loves me ev'ry day the same,
Even calls me by my name.

Day by day, at home, away,
Jesus is my staff and stay.
When I hunger, Jesus feeds me,
Into pleasant pastures leads me;
When I thirst, He bids me go
Where the quiet waters flow.

Who so happy as I am,
Even now the Shepherd's lamb?
And when my short life is ended,
By His angel host attended,
He shall fold me to His breast,
There within His arms to rest.

(*All God's People Sing*, 125)

My Family

Parents serve God and their children in four vital areas of life:

- Physical health
- Mental health
- Social health
- Spiritual well-being

Parents are given the responsibility to provide food, clothes, shelter, and medical and dental care for children.

Parents arrange for their children's education. They help with homework, offer instruction, and provide guidance.

Parents will see that their children are taught social graces and manners—how to be polite. They provide opportunities for their children to make good friends and encourage their children to be concerned about and care for others.

Parents should pray for their children, read God's Word and have devotions with them, take them to church and Sunday school, and, as possible, send their children to a Christian school.

The best families are those where parents and children know, love, respect, and care for each other.

Check it out! Read Ephesians 6:4.

What expectations does God have of parents according to this passage?

....

....

....

....

....

....

....

....

....

....

Finally, brothers,
whatever is true, whatever is noble,
whatever is right, whatever is pure,
whatever is lovely, whatever is
admirable—if anything is
excellent or praiseworthy—
think about such things.
Whatever you have learned
or received or heard from me,
or seen in me—put it into practice.
And the God of peace will be with you.
Philippians 4:8–9

Picture this! Traditionally, a family was symbolized by a father, mother, and children, often a boy and a girl—the "ideal" family. Today families come in many shapes and sizes. What might be an appropriate symbol for your family?

Hard Questions!

What if I can't honor my dad or mom?

Some children—adult children too—have special concerns. Perhaps their parents abused them. Perhaps they grew up in violent homes. Perhaps their parents failed to show support, concern, or even love. When parents neglect or abuse their children, they are obviously not living up to God's expectations.

So what should we do?

- Love the abusing parent. It may be hard, but they need love, as well as honor and respect. They need your prayers. Follow Jesus' example of loving the sinner but despising the sin.

- Confide in someone who can help: a pastor, a favorite teacher, a trusted adult. It is important that the abusive situation be confronted, and where possible, corrected by responsible authorities.

- When your goal is to build up, your intentions are good. If your motive is revenge, destruction, and hurt, you are breaking the Fourth Commandment.

- If a friend is in an abusive relationship, be supportive and encouraging. As possible, help the person to get out of a dangerous situation.

How do we as God's redeemed people in Christ Jesus honor Him with respect at those times when we find it difficult to honor those in authority over us at home, school, work, in government, or at church?

My Friends
Hard Questions!

What about my friends who are not Christian?

It's often painful when you have a friend who doesn't believe in God. They may be among your very best friends, and you'd like to think that they would go to heaven.

God's Word says, of course, there is only one way to be saved:

"Salvation is found in no one else, for there is no other name under heaven given to men by which we must be saved" (Acts 4:12).

Ultimately, we have to trust the grace and mercy of God.

What can you do now?

- Pray for them. Invite others to pray for them.

- Be a good friend to them. Encourage them.

- Don't hide your faith and don't be afraid to mention it.

- Be consistent with your faith. Be a witness to what you believe. Live your faith.

- Invite your friend to church and youth activities. Help him or her to always feel welcome.

- When the opportunity arises, actually talk about Jesus.

Check it out! Read Exodus 16.

How does God reveal His care for His people?

....

....

....

....

....

....

....

....

....

....

....

....

Confirmation Remembered

In You is Gladness

In You is gladness Amid all sadness,
Jesus, sunshine of my heart.
By You are given The gifts of heaven,
You the true Redeemer are.
Our souls are waking; Our bonds are breaking.
Who trusts You surely Has built securely
And stands forever. Alleluia!
Our hearts are pining To see Your shining,
Dying or living To You are cleaving
Now and forever. Alleluia!

If he is ours, We fear no powers,
Not of earth or sin or death.
He sees and blesses In worst distresses;
He can change them with a breath.
Wherefore the story Tell of His glory
With hearts and voices; All heav'n rejoices
In Him forever. Alleluia!
We shout for gladness, Win over sadness,
Love Him and praise Him
And still shall raise Him
Glad hymns forever. Alleluia!

(Lutheran Worship, 442)

What do your friends think about God? What would they think of you if you started to talk about God in your conversations?

. . . .

. . . .

. . . .

. . . .

. . . .

. . . .

. . . .

. . . .

. . . .

. . . .

. . . .

Rejoice in the Lord always.
I will say it again: Rejoice!
Let your gentleness be evident to all.
The Lord is near.
Do not be anxious about anything,
but in everything,
by prayer and petition,
with thanksgiving,
present your requests to God.
And the peace of God,
which transcends all understanding,
will guard your hearts
and your minds in Christ Jesus.
Philippians 4:4–7